KEN GRIFFEY SR.
AND
KEN GRIFFEY JR.

BASEBALL HEROES

J. Elizabeth Mills

rosen publishing's
rosen
central

New York

To my brother Michael—A true sportsman

Published in 2010 by The Rosen Publishing Group, Inc.
29 East 21st Street, New York, NY 10010

Library of Congress Cataloging-in-Publication Data

Mills, J. Elizabeth.
Ken Griffey Sr. and Ken Griffey Jr.: baseball heroes / J. Elizabeth Mills.—1st ed.
    p. cm.—(Sports families)
Includes bibliographical references and index.
ISBN 978-1-4358-3554-2 (library binding)
ISBN 978-1-4358-8514-1 (pbk)
ISBN 978-1-4358-8515-8 (6 pack)
1. Griffey, Ken, 1950-–Juvenile literature. 2. Griffey, Ken, Jr.—Juvenile literature. 3. Baseball players—United States—Biography—Juvenile literature. I. Title.
GV865.A1M55 2010
796.3570922--dc22

2009017006

Manufactured in the United States of America

CPSIA Compliance Information: Batch #LW10YA: For Further Information contact Rosen Publishing, New York, New York at 1-800-237-9932

On the cover: Ken Griffey Sr. and Ken Griffey Jr. have shared more than just the same birthplace—they've also shared a season in which they hit back-to-back home runs, a first in Major League Baseball history!

On the back cover: NASCAR is a registered trademark of the National Association for Stock Car Auto Racing, Inc.

Contents

A true father-and-son team, Ken Griffey Sr. and Ken Griffey Jr. have supported each other through good times and bad, home runs and injuries. They are best friends.

It was a cool summer evening on August 31, 1990, as huge crowds of people swarmed into the Seattle Kingdome. The air was full of the smell of hot dogs and fries and the sounds of excited fans and shouting drink vendors. This was no ordinary night of baseball. For the first time in the history of professional baseball, a father and son were going to play on the same team.

The players took the field. The crowd roared. Ken Griffey Jr. wore his cap backward, as he had done since he wore his father's cap as a young boy. What a night this would be. They had played catch together for years. Junior had watched Senior bat in the minor leagues and then in the majors for the Cincinnati Reds. Senior had cheered Junior on through Little League, high school varsity, the minor leagues, and then through his first year with the Seattle Mariners.

Now, in front of thousands of fans, on a cool summer night, these two friends who shared a passion for baseball were going to have the time of their lives.

The game began. Senior was second in the batting order. In the bottom of the first inning, he bashed the ball through the middle. Junior was up next and hit the ball hard to right field. The duo had gotten back-to-back hits. The fans were thrilled. After the game, Ken Senior and Ken Junior celebrated this new chapter in their careers. For the first time, they would be able to watch each other play in person and support each other.

Two weeks later, in Anaheim, California, the Griffeys made history again with back-to-back home runs. Senior smacked the pitch into the left center bleacher seats. Then, a home run from Junior landed not far from where his father's had gone. They were having a blast.

Chapter One

THE JUNIOR YEARS

George Kenneth Griffey Jr. was born on November 21, 1969, in Donora, Pennsylvania, a town not far from Pittsburgh. His parents are Ken Griffey Sr. and Alberta (Bertie) Griffey. He has one brother, Craig. Ken Griffey Jr. never went by George. Most folks knew him as Little Kenny or Junior. His father is called Big Kenny.

The year Junior was born, his father signed a contract to play in the minor leagues. Each Major League Baseball (MLB) team has a set of smaller minor league teams, often called farm teams, whose players train and play games and get ready to move up into the major leagues. But the pay is not as good in the minor leagues, and Ken Griffey Sr.'s family often did not have much money in those first few years.

Then, in 1973, Ken Sr. got the call he had been waiting for. He would start as an outfielder for the Cincinnati Reds! The whole family was very excited. They moved to Mount Airy, Ohio. On August 25, 1973, in his major league debut, Ken Sr. was sixth in the batting lineup. He hit a ground ball in his first at bat, which was caught and thrown to first for an out. In his second at bat, Ken hit a double and then later a single. He went two for four that night.

The Cincinnati Reds of the 1970s were called the Big Red Machine, winning six division titles and two World Series. Ken Sr. played in two World Series championships during this decade, one in 1975 and the other in 1976. Ken Sr. would continue to play for the Reds through 1981.

Ken Griffey Sr. played for the Big Red Machine in Cincinnati, Ohio, from 1973 to 1981, and then again from 1988 to 1990.

Although Junior grew up watching his father play baseball, his dad cared more about having fun with Junior and the other kids in the neighborhood. Ken Sr. played basketball and football with Ken Jr. and Craig, as well as baseball. When the Reds were in town, Junior would hang out at Riverfront Stadium to watch batting practice and then watch part of the game from the stands. Ken Jr. found it hard to sit still for a long time, and after a bit, he would go meet other kids whose dads played for the Reds—Pete Rose Jr. and Victor and Eduardo Perez. They would play their own game under the stadium.

The Griffey father-and-son duo enjoyed playing together for 51 games during 1990 and 1991. Their relationship made for a unique team dynamic.

LITTLE LEAGUE

When Junior was eight, he started Little League. And it was clear early on that he had his father's talent for the sport. He had a good arm and pitched hard fastballs to the batters at the plate. He even made some of them cry because his pitches were so fast. In one game, the coach on the opposing team demanded to see Junior's birth certificate, not believing he was the right age. Luckily, the Griffeys lived close to the field, and Junior's mother, Bertie, ran home to get the document. Junior really was nine, and the game was allowed to continue.

According to Junior, his father taught him how to hit. Rather than pitch underhand, a common way to throw to kids, his father pitched overhand, just like in real baseball games. So Junior learned to hit all kinds of pitches at a young age. Junior also threw the ball to his dad for batting practice. Once, while his father was recovering from knee surgery, he asked Junior to pitch to him. Afraid of hurting his father, Junior avoided pitching close to his father's body. But it's important to know how to pitch inside. So his father pushed him and pushed him. Eventually, Junior threw the ball correctly and hit his father on the knee. Though his father was in pain, he was proud of his son, and Junior had overcome his fear.

Junior enjoyed playing baseball, but he also put a lot of pressure on himself to do well. He hit long home runs and played quite a few games without ever getting a strikeout. Then at last it happened. And he got very upset. Even though his mother told him that everyone strikes out, including his father, Junior pointed out that he was not his father. He did not want to cause outs and get strikes. He resolved to work harder and practice more. Junior dreamed of one day playing for a big team like his dad.

MORE TO LIFE THAN JUST BASEBALL

Junior learned more than just baseball from his dad. He also learned important life lessons. He liked to show off and make people laugh. In a talent show at school, Junior decided to mimic famous baseball players and their bat swings. His father was not pleased. He told Junior to find his own style and stick with it, not try and profit from other people's successes. Senior wanted his son to be himself, to go out onto the field and have a good time. He taught his son to play well and not show off. He would be appreciated for his talent, not for his bragging. Ken Sr. was out of town a lot and often missed his son's games. So Bertie would record them and send the tapes to Ken Sr. so he could watch them in the evening. He would give his son tips based on the recordings. Occasionally, he was able to come to a live game. Usually, he wouldn't tell anyone he was

Even though Ken Griffey Sr. was far away in New York, he still followed his son's Little League career by watching recordings and talking to his family.

coming so that he would not be mobbed by fans. But Junior knew he was there, and he would put so much pressure on himself that often he wouldn't play well.

In 1981, Ken Sr. was traded to New York to play first base and outfield for the Yankees. Now he would see even fewer of his son's games. Instead, they talked on the phone all the time. Ken Sr. would even fly his son to New York to scold him when he did something wrong. He wanted his son to feel he still had a dad.

In high school, Junior played both football and baseball. He wanted to be a star immediately, so he put all his energy into sports. He was a wide receiver on the football team, as well as a punter and kicker. He became a center fielder for the school's baseball team. Unfortunately, he did not do his schoolwork and his grades went down. As a result, he could not play at all for the first two years of high school. His father was very angry. He told his son that it was unlikely he would make it into the major leagues, so he needed to pay attention in school and get good grades. Junior understood. He focused on his schoolwork, brought up his grades, and was allowed to play sports again. He grew to 6 foot 3 inches (190 centimeters) and gained weight so that he was 180 pounds (81 kilograms). His physical strength helped immensely on the field. At age 16, he joined the Connie Mack League, which usually takes 18-year-olds, and took the team to

BASEBALL STATISTICS

Baseball is a game of numbers and averages. These numbers and averages are called statistics. Fans and players use these numbers to judge a player's performance.

When a player comes to the plate, it's called an at bat. The player can do a number of things. He can get a hit, which is called a single if he is safe at first base, a double if he makes it to second base, and a triple if he makes it to third. He can get a strike, meaning the ball is not played. He can get a home run, which means he has hit the ball so far either in the park or out of park that the ball cannot be caught or played. Lastly, he can be "walked," which means the pitcher has thrown four pitches outside of the strike zone and the player can move to first without hitting the ball.

Batting average is calculated by dividing the number of hits a player has by the number of at bats, or times the player has come up to bat. This average measures a player's batting ability.

A batting average of .500 means that a batter gets a hit half the time he's at bat. A batting average of .330 means a player gets a hit one in three times at bat. This is a very good batting average. Most players have batting averages at or above .300.

the Connie Mack World Series. He hit a home run to center field, one to left field, and one to right field in the championship game.

But Junior excelled at football, too. The University of Oklahoma liked Junior and wanted him to come play for their school. Ken Sr. told his son that he would have to choose. Junior chose baseball, knowing he could turn professional right after high school.

Junior was excited to be in the big leagues, but he faced a lot of pressure to succeed from his family, teammates, fans, and himself.

Meanwhile, his father was battling injuries with the Yankees. In 1986, Ken Sr. was traded again, this time to Atlanta, where he played for only one complete season. Then he returned to Cincinnati to play the 1989 season. At this point, Ken Sr. was nearly 40 years old, and he wasn't sure how many games he would have left as a professional baseball player.

In his senior year of high school, Junior had a .474 batting average, with 7 home runs, 28 runs batted in, and 13 stolen bases, all in just 24 games. For the second year in a row, he was named most valuable player for the Greater Catholic League. Scouts—people sent by major league teams to find new players—were very interested in Junior and thought he would be a top prospect for the 1987 draft.

Sure enough, Ken Griffey Jr. was selected in the first round of the MLB draft in 1987 by the Seattle Mariners. Junior was off to the major leagues!

Chapter Two

Just Having Fun

Junior was excited to play for the Seattle Mariners. But first he would have to prove himself in the minor leagues. Two days after graduation, he moved to Bellingham, Washington, to play for the Mariners' Single-A team. Junior boasted he would be playing for the Mariners within a year.

Junior soon realized, however, that the minor leagues have their own challenges. He encountered pitches he had never seen before. He played in five games without getting a single hit. Finally, he hit a home run against Everett, Washington. Junior felt a little better, but he knew he was a long way from home. His batting average was just .230.

As the months went by, Junior began to find his rhythm again. By the middle of summer, his batting average had soared to .453, and in 16 games, he had 7 home runs and 16 runs batted in (RBIs). He ended the season with an overall average of .313. He held team records in batting average, home runs, and RBIs.

But Junior wasn't having as much fun. He felt intense pressure to succeed, since he was a first-round draft pick. Even when he went home, the pressure continued. His father expected him to be an adult, but Junior just wanted to escape. One night, Junior swallowed almost 300 aspirin tablets. He was upset and angry and wanted to do something. Fortunately, a family friend drove him to the hospital where doctors pumped his stomach. Later, Junior regretted trying to take his life and spoke about the experience with other teens to help them understand the importance of their lives. Best of all, Junior and his father took time to reconnect and find the bond they once had.

When Junior returned to the minor leagues, he played in San Bernardino, California, and then in Vermont for the Double-A team in August 1988. He blasted homers and impressed the Mariners' coaches, who wanted to move him up to Triple-A in spring in Canada. Junior thought differently. At spring training the next season, Junior put on a show. He flew through the outfield, making incredible catches and consistently got hits and home runs. The coaches knew they had a star. The Mariners' manager, Jim Lefebvre, told Junior he would be the starting center fielder for the Seattle Mariners. Junior called his dad to share the great news.

THE BIG TIME

On April 2, 1989, Ken Griffey Jr. walked up to home plate for his first major league at bat in Oakland Coliseum wearing number 24. He was the youngest player in the league, but he wasted no time showing why he was there. He hit a double off the second pitch and streaked to second base. It was an exciting evening. But the magic wouldn't last. Junior didn't get a hit in the next five games and began to worry that he would be sent back to the minors. He talked to his father and shared his fears. Ken Sr. told his son to be patient and keep playing. In time, he would find a new rhythm.

His father was right. At the Mariners' home opener on April 10, 1989, Junior watched as the fans stood to welcome their new player. He sent the first pitch flying over the fence in left field—his first major league home run. Junior called it his father's birthday present. Over the next few games, Junior tied records and made new ones. He was loved by the fans for his smile, his talent, and his friendly nature.

The amazing thing about Ken Griffey Jr. was that he refused to spend time getting to know the pitchers he faced. Most players watch videos and

When Junior played his first game with the Seattle Mariners in 1989, he was the youngest player in the league.

study how pitchers throw to find a way to beat them. But Ken wanted to just go out there and have fun. Baseball was a game to him, and he made it look easy. By July, he had hit 13 home runs and made some incredibly acrobatic catches. Fans began to hope that Junior would take the Mariners to their first World Series. But no player goes without an injury. Junior broke a finger when he fell in a hotel shower and was unable to play for a month. The Mariners suffered without their star player and did not make the playoffs. Junior finished the season with a respectable .264 batting average, having scored 16 home runs, stolen 16 bases, and gotten 61 runs and RBIs.

The following season, Junior started his streak early. In April, he led the league in batting average (.388), home runs (5), and RBIs (17). He was chosen as American League Player of the Month. He excelled in the outfield, too, denying home runs and making spectacular plays. Manager Lefebvre called Junior "the Kid." Junior liked the nickname so much that he put it on the license plate of his car.

The Mariners still struggled, though, despite Junior's talent, and so the management signed Ken Griffey Sr. For the first time ever, a father and son pair would play together on the same field. The experience was magical for the Griffeys, and though the Mariners had another losing season, hopes were high for 1991. Junior was given the Gold Glove award for defensive excellence, the second youngest recipient of the award. Since then, he has received the Gold Glove every season.

But in the spring of 1991, Ken Griffey Sr. was in a car accident. At the age of 41, he was no longer able to bounce back from his injuries, and he decided to retire midseason. Junior was very upset. He had hoped to continue to play alongside his father. Junior's performance suffered for a while. But the fans still loved him and voted him into the All-Star Game. He received more votes than anyone else in the American League. The game lifted his spirits, and he finished the season with a .327 batting average, 42 doubles, and 3 grand slams. Junior also received the Silver Bat award, given to the batting champions of the American and National leagues. He won the award three more times, in 1993, 1994, and 1996.

The manager of the Seattle Mariners, Jim Lefebvre, was one of Junior's biggest fans, calling him "The Kid."

PLAYOFF HOPES

More ups and downs came in 1992. Ken Griffey Jr. and his fiancée, Melissa, were married. Junior's favorite manager, Jim Lefebvre, was fired and the

THE CINCINNATI RED STOCKINGS

In 1869, when organized baseball was still young, a group called the Cincinnati Baseball Club, nicknamed the Red Stockings, became the first professional team. They traveled throughout the country playing and defeating semipro and amateur teams, going undefeated 57–0 for the season. These players were the ambassadors of a new game called baseball. Nowadays, a group re-creates the game as it was once played, educating and entertaining the public about America's favorite pastime.

new manager, Bill Plummer, did not provide the Mariners with good leadership. The team finished last with a record of 64–98. Plummer, too, was fired. But Junior went to his second straight All-Star Game, in San Diego, where he got a single, a double, and a home run. He was named the All-Star Game Most Valuable Player, an award his father had won in 1980.

The following year, Junior improved in many ways. Not only did his statistics go up, but his strength increased, too. He was blasting his homers way past the wall, 45 of them by the end of the year. On June 15, 1993, Junior hit his 100th home run off of Kansas City pitcher Billy Brewer. He was the sixth-youngest player to do so. In July, Junior went on an eight-game hitting streak, which tied a major league record. All in all, it was a good year for Junior, especially in the off-season, when his son, Trey Kenneth, was born on January 19, 1994.

The 1994 season began with a bang. By the time May ended, Junior had hit 22 home runs, breaking a record of 20 held by Mickey Mantle. By the end of June, he had hit 32, breaking Babe Ruth's record of 30. He received more votes to the All-Star Game than any player had ever

Fans did their best to protest the possibility of a strike in the days leading up to the season-ending decision.

received. And once there, he won the Home Run Derby. By August, he had hit 40 home runs.

But then the season came to a crashing halt. There was an argument over how to spend the league's money. Players and owners couldn't agree. So the players went on strike, and the season was canceled, as was the World Series. Fans all over were confused and sad. There was no baseball to watch for the rest of 1994. Eventually, the argument was settled, and the 1995 season started, though two weeks late.

The Mariners were more than ready to get to work. On Opening Day, Junior hit a three-run homer to win the game. He played his best this year, and the other players and coaches knew it. But the high point would not last. The Mariners were fighting for the top spot in the division in May, when Griffey made a spectacular and devastating catch. He fractured two bones in his left wrist and had to have emergency surgery to insert a metal plate in his wrist. He sat in the dugout for the next three months, watching helplessly as the Mariners fell from first place. But as soon as he had healed, he grabbed his bat and got back to work. The Mariners went on a tear, winning game after game. They made it into the playoffs against the New York Yankees. Junior had done it.

The Mariners lost games 1 and 2, despite Junior's hits and RBIs and homers. Playing in Seattle for game 3, Junior and fellow teammate Edgar Martinez together hit homers to save the game. Game 5 was do-or-die. The Yankees were leading 4–2 in the eighth inning. Fans were cheering, desperately hoping their star could make a miracle happen. Junior came to the plate and belted a home run to bring the score to 4–3. It was his fifth in the playoffs, which tied the record for most playoff home runs in a series. The Mariners tied up the game and sent it into extra innings. Down again by one in the 11th inning, Griffey got on base with a single. One runner, Joey Cora, advanced to second. Martinez got a single and the runners advanced again, with Cora tying the game. But Griffey didn't stop running. He ran from first base all the way home, winning the game. The team jumped on top of him at home plate. The Mariners had won!

Unfortunately, the Mariners lost in the next round to the Cleveland Indians, but the fans still considered the season a success. The Mariners had made the playoffs, and Junior had worked his magic.

On October 21, 1995, Junior and Melissa had a daughter, Taryn Kennedy. The family moved to Florida, their off-season home state, and lived in a

Junior had an incredible season in 1996. He set batting records on the field and gave back to his community off the field.

house that Junior designed with his love of sports in mind. There's a golf course, a lake, a playroom, and a mini movie theater!

In January 1996, Junior extended his contract with the Mariners for four years, earning $34 million. He appeared on commercial products as well, including a box of Honey Frosted Wheaties, the first player ever to do so. He also received the Roberto Clemente Award for outstanding community service.

Junior continued to set franchise records in the 1996 season, with 49 home runs and 140 RBIs. In May 1996, he hit career home run number 200 off of Boston Red Sox pitcher Vaughn Eshelman. But he got injured again midseason with a broken wrist bone, causing him to miss three weeks. But that didn't stop the fans from voting him into his seventh straight All-Star Game.

In the 1997 playoffs, the Mariners lost to the Orioles. But Junior was voted the league's Most Valuable Player and finished the season with 56 home runs.

Chapter Three

THE HOME RUN KING

The 1998 season started the Great Home Run Race. The press began to talk about Roger Maris's record of 61 home runs in one season. Two other star baseball players, Mark McGwire and Sammy Sosa, were trying to beat Maris's record. When asked if he was also trying to beat the record, Junior insisted that he just wanted to focus on getting back to the playoffs. But he kept hitting home runs and the press kept asking questions. Eventually, he finished the season with 56. McGwire hit 70, and Sosa hit 66. Junior hit home run number 300 on April 13, 1998, against the Cleveland Indians' pitcher Jose Mesa. He was the second youngest player to hit the 300 mark. Unfortunately, the Mariners did not make it to the playoffs in 1998 or in 1999.

Griffey was frustrated. He wanted to be in the playoffs. He wanted to win, the way his father had won. He also wanted to be closer to his family. He requested to be traded and was thrilled to learn that he would be playing for the Cincinnati Reds—his father's team. The city of Cincinnati was equally happy that their son was coming home. Hopes were high that he would take the team to the World Series.

When he got to Cincinnati, Junior took his father's jersey number, 30. He was also reunited with his father, the bench coach for the Reds. On April 11, 2000, Junior hit his 400th career home run on his father's 50th birthday, continuing a tradition that started with his rookie home run back in 1989. He has hit eight home runs on his dad's birthday.

Baseball fans were obsessed with the home run race in 1998 between Mark McGwire and Sammy Sosa. It was a very exciting time for Major League Baseball.

INJURIES

Junior led the Reds to a winning season, but it would be the last. Junior endured injury after injury to his hamstrings and his knees, as well as negative reactions from teammates and fans. He played just 181 games in 2001 and 2002 combined, and hit only 30 home runs. He lost his smile and easy attitude. Fans began saying mean things to his family in the stands, suggesting that they return to Seattle. His father also suddenly left his post as bench coach and later hitting coach, choosing instead to assist the general manager Jim Bowden.

Junior did his best to stay positive and mentor the young players around him. He continued his charity work, flying kids out from Orlando- and Seattle-area Boys & Girls Clubs to Ohio to attend some games and go to an amusement park. Most fans do not know that he is on the national board of directors for the Boys & Girls Clubs of America and has been a part of the Make-a-Wish Foundation since his rookie year. In 1994, Junior received an award from the Make-a-Wish Foundation for his generous contributions and genuine care for others. He and Melissa also adopted their third child, a boy named Tevin, in 2002.

On the field, however, Junior was continuing to have trouble. In 2003, he dislocated his right shoulder and tore an ankle tendon. In 2004, he tore

Ken Griffey Sr. served as bench coach for the Cincinnati Reds, providing support and advice to the ballplayers. The bench coach is second-in-command to the team's manager.

his right hamstring a second time. All of these injuries required lengthy rehabilitation, meaning he missed even more games—260 out of 486 games between 2002 and 2004.

Home Runs 500 and 600

Things started to look up in 2004 when, on June 20, he hit home run 500 off of the Arizona Cardinals' pitcher Matt Morris. It was Father's Day, and he went right over to his dad after crossing home plate and wished him a happy Father's Day. That was his fourth career home run on Father's Day.

Junior gave his father the perfect Father's Day present on June 20, 2004, by scoring a home run—the 500th of his career!

The same year, Ken Griffey Sr. was also inducted into the Cincinnati Reds Hall of Fame. But right before the All-Star break, Junior got injured again, partially tearing a hamstring, which took him out of the All-Star Game and put him back on the disabled list. This partial tear turned into a complete separation of the hamstring from his leg bone during a game in San Francisco, with Junior ending 2004 back on the disabled list. Doctors performed a special experimental surgery in which three titanium screws were implanted to hold the hamstring in place. Junior's leg was held in a sling at a 90-degree angle, unable to be moved, until October. Once he completed rehabilitation, he returned to play the 2005 season.

In April, his batting average was .244 with one home run and nine RBIs. Griffey seemed to have regained his strength. He hit 35 home runs, the most since 2000. But then in September, he strained a tendon in his left foot. Since the Reds would not make the playoffs, the team decided to keep him on the bench so that he could have necessary surgeries completed on various injuries. In all, though, he played 128 games in 2005, the most since he had arrived with the Reds, and he was named National League Comeback Player of the Year.

In the off-season, he played for the American team in the World Baseball Classic with his father as the coach. Junior's batting average was .524, but the U.S. team did not reach the semifinals.

The 2006 season was relatively injury-free, and he continued to move up the ladder with career home runs. In 2007, Junior changed his number from 30 to 3 in honor of this three children. He hit home run after home run, with number 573 coming on May 22. Then on June 22, 2007, Junior went back to Seattle for the first time since the trade to play four games with the Mariners. He was unsure how he would be received. But he had no reason to worry. Fans packed the stands, the Mariners honored him with a film about his career in Seattle, the team presented him with a "The House That Griffey Built" memorial, and there was a four-minute standing ovation—all for Ken Griffey Jr., still a fan favorite. Junior was very grateful, and he hit two more home runs during the series.

LITTLE LEAGUE BASEBALL

In 1939, Little League Baseball was founded in Pennsylvania by a man named Carl Stotz, who wanted to organize a baseball league for the local boys. He tried out different kinds of equipment and field sizes, but the group had no name and no teams. In 1939, three teams were established: Lycoming Dairy, Lundy Lumber, and Jumbo Pretzel. The name became Little League. The first game was played on June 6, 1939, between Lundy Lumber and Lycoming Dairy. The league expanded within the United States and then around the world, and soon Little League became the largest organized youth sports program in the world.

Little League Baseball oversees more than 7,000 children's baseball leagues with more than 2.2 million participants in the United States and around the world.

Once again receiving the most fan votes to go to the All-Star Game, Junior did not disappoint, sending in two runs for the National League. On August 22, 2007, Junior received an all-time Gold Glove award, along with nine other players who were thought to be the best defensive players in the last half-century. But sadly, this season would also end in injury with a groin strain in September. His stats in 2007 included 78 runs, 24 doubles, 1 triple, 30 home runs, 93 RBIs, and a .277 batting average.

Junior's first home run of the 2008 season came in a victory over the Philadelphia Phillies on April 6. It was his 594th career home run. Two months later, on June 9, in front of his family and 16,003 fans, Ken Griffey Jr. hit home run 600 off of the Florida Marlins' pitcher Mark Hendrickson in Dolphin Stadium. The ball sailed far into the night, and Junior flew around the bases to a standing ovation. He had hit home runs off of 383 different pitchers and now had 600 homers under his belt.

But on August 7, Junior was traded to the Chicago White Sox. Batting just .245 with 15 homers and 53 RBIs, Junior was not the player he once was. He has never been back to the playoffs since he left the Mariners and has never won a World Series. Chicago was looking to add him to their roster so that he could lead them to a championship. But Junior was soon plagued by yet another injury, and the White Sox were eliminated from the postseason. Junior ended the 2008 season with 611 career home runs.

Junior hit his 600th career home run, joining all-time greats Babe Ruth, Hank Aaron, Willie Mays, Sammy Sosa, and Barry Bonds.

On February 19, 2009, the Seattle Mariners announced that Junior would be going back to Seattle, under a one-year contract. It's been a long, hard road, but the Kid is home.

Chapter Four

A BRIGHT FUTURE

Junior's father has been busy with his charity work. The Ken Griffey Sr. Foundation works to promote healthy lifestyles and physical fitness to young people. Ken Sr. believes that important skills, such as teamwork and leadership, can be learned through baseball and wants to promote baseball to inner-city youth. The foundation also helps spread information on how to combat and/or avoid childhood obesity and adult obesity through a lifestyle built around exercise and proper diet.

Ken is a board member of an organization called Zero Cancer, whose mission is to promote early detection and increased research efforts. Ken was recently diagnosed with prostate cancer. Fortunately, the cancer was caught in its early stages and treated. He is now a survivor, and he uses his celebrity status to advocate for many charities, including the National Prostate Cancer Coalition. Ken's wife, Bertie, was also diagnosed with cancer. She has been treated, and the cancer is now in remission.

Last year, Ken's former hometown of Donora, Pennsylvania, honored him at a banquet to dedicate the Ken Griffey Sr. Field. Ken has taken good care of his hometown and its school district, where he was inducted into the Mid-Mon Valley All Sports Hall of Fame in 1973, at age 23. In high school, Ken played basketball and football. The Ringgold school board approved the field dedication to Ken Griffey Sr., who has also supported the Mon Valley YMCA.

Ken Griffey Sr.'s foundation is dedicated to promoting healthy living through sports and nutrition to young people all over the United States.

Ken Griffey Sr. also spends part of his time as special consultant to the general manager of the Cincinnati Reds, Wayne Krivsky, and as a talent scout.

KEN GRIFFEY JR.

Ken Griffey Jr.'s life has been about as full off the field as it has been on the field. His family and his charity work are a large part of his time and focus when he's not playing baseball.

On June 17, 2008, Ken Griffey Jr. donated the helmet he wore when he hit home run number 600 to the Baseball Hall of Fame.

When Trey was born in 1993, Woody Woodward, the general manager of the Mariners at the time, sent Junior a player's contract for Trey that was dated 2012, jokingly implying Trey would follow in his father's footsteps. Trey does play baseball, but he enjoys football as well, and he says his dream is to become a star football player. At 15, he is almost as tall as his father and he has big hands. He plays running back and linebacker. Junior's daughter, Taryn, plays AAU basketball and is a star point guard. And the youngest, Tevin, participates in Pop Warner basketball and football. Junior is happy that his kids are finding their way. In a *Sports Illustrated* interview, Junior said, "I just tell them that I'll always be proud of them, no matter what. I just want them to be themselves." It is a lesson Junior learned from his dad and one that has served him well.

Just as Junior's dad watched videotapes of his son's games when he was on the road, now Junior watches online footage of his kids' activities when he's not in town. He gives them tips and comments, continuing the Griffey tradition. But when he is in town, he involves the family in all kinds of activities, like bowling and go-kart racing. Like his father, he wants to be as much a part of his children's lives as he can, while still playing professional baseball.

COMMERCIAL PLAY

Many famous sports figures receive endorsements, or money, from brand-name products to feature a player's name or photo on a package. In the case of Ken Griffey Jr., some products were successful, others were not. For one year, there was a chocolate candy bar named after him, called the Ken Griffey Jr. Bar. About a million bars were sold, but unfortunately, Junior was allergic to chocolate. The bar was discontinued. In 1996, Nike endorsed Junior, creating an ad campaign centered around "Ken Griffey Jr. for President." Nike created "Griffey in '96" buttons and a TV commercial. Realistically, Junior could not have taken office for many reasons, but the main reason was that he was only 26 years old! Junior has starred in four Nintendo video games. He had a guest role on *The Simpsons* and *The Fresh Prince of Bel-Air*.

Junior knows that one day he'll have to retire, but until then, he plans on having a good time and enjoying the game as long as he can. In the meantime, he sets up all kinds of charity events, including golf tournaments and bowling tournaments, through his organization—The Ken Griffey Jr. Family Foundation—to benefit children's hospitals, Boys & Girls Clubs, and other recipients. He continues to look for ways to give back to the fans who gave him so much devotion and affection during his many years in the majors.

On November 18, 2008, then secretary of state Condoleezza Rice appointed several famous people, including Ken Griffey Jr., Cal Ripken Jr., and Michelle Kwan to be public diplomacy envoys for America. The position would enable them to travel throughout the world, promoting

Ken Griffey Jr. is only the third athlete to be named a public diplomacy envoy.

interest in America, spreading peace, and connecting with other countries through common interests, such as sports. Junior's prominence in a well-recognized sport makes him an excellent candidate for this position and a terrific role model.

1969

George Kenneth Griffey Jr. is born in Donora, Pennsylvania. Ken Griffey Sr. signs a contract to play in the minor leagues.

1973

Ken Griffey Sr. is called up to the major leagues to play outfield for the Cincinnati Reds. The family moves to Mount Airy, Ohio.

1977

Junior plays his first year in Little League. Senior homers and wins the All-Star Game.

1981

Senior is traded to the New York Yankees.

1983

At Moeller High School, Junior plays football and baseball.

1987

Ken Griffey Jr. is selected as first-round draft pick by the Seattle Mariners. Junior plays for the Mariners' Single-A team in Bellingham, Washington.

1988

Junior starts his second minor league season at San Bernardino, California.

1989

Junior makes his major league debut at the Oakland Coliseum against the Oakland Athletics. Junior meets Melissa, his future wife.

1990

Ken Griffey Sr. and Ken Griffey Jr. make history as the first father-son pair to play together on the same field in the major leagues. Junior wins his first Gold Glove award with his stellar defense.

1991

Ken Griffey Sr. is in a car accident and is forced to retire. Junior receives more votes by fans for the All-Star Game than any other American Leaguer.

1992

Junior and Melissa are married. They move to Issaquah, Washington.

1993

Junior homers in eight straight games, tying a major league record. Junior's son, Trey Kenneth, is born. Junior receives an award from the Make-a-Wish Foundation for his generosity and "caring for fellow citizens."

1994

Junior hits 32 home runs by the end of June, breaking Babe Ruth's record of 30. The players strike, and the season is canceled. Junior wins the Home Run Derby during the All-Star Game.

1996

Junior becomes the first baseball player to appear on a box of Honey Frosted Wheaties. Junior goes to his seventh straight All-Star Game.

1997

Mariners win the division title but do not advance in the playoffs.

1998

Mariners fail to win again. Griffey hits home run number 300. He is the second youngest player to reach 300. Griffey goes to the All-Star Game.

1999

Junior is one of 30 players named to Major League Baseball's All-Century team. At 29, he is the youngest player selected.

2000

Junior is traded to the Cincinnati Reds. Senior wears number 33 as the bench coach for the Reds. Later, he becomes the hitting coach. Junior hits home run number 400 on his father's 50th birthday.

2002

Senior resigns and is now a special assistant to the general manager.

2004

Junior hits home run number 500 on Father's Day.

2008

Junior is traded to the Chicago White Sox as a center fielder. Secretary of State Condoleeza Rice names Ken Griffey Jr. a public diplomacy envoy.

2009

The Seattle Mariners announce that Ken Griffey Jr. is coming back to Seattle to play for the Mariners in the 2009 season.

GLOSSARY

at bat An official turn at batting charged to a baseball player except when the player walks, sacrifices, is hit by a pitched ball, or is interfered with by the catcher.

batting average A ratio of base hits to official times at bat for a baseball player.

center fielder The player defending center field.

double A base hit that allows the batter to reach second base.

envoy A person delegated to represent one government in its dealings with another.

fastball A baseball pitch thrown at full speed and often rising slightly as it nears the plate.

groin The fold or depression marking the juncture of the lower abdomen and the inner part of the thigh.

hamstring One of two groups of tendons at the back of the thigh.

home run A hit in baseball that enables the batter to make a complete circuit of the bases and score a run.

major league A league of highest classification in U.S. professional baseball.

minor league A league of professional clubs in a sport other than the recognized major leagues.

outfielder A player who occupies a baseball defensive position comprising right field, center field, or left field.

pitcher The player who throws the ball to the batter.

punter The person who punts the ball in football.

run A score made in baseball by a runner reaching home plate safely.

runs batted in A statistic that credits a batter whose at bat results in a run being scored.

single A base hit that allows the batter to reach first base.

statistics A collection of quantitative data.

strike A pitched ball that is in the strike zone or is swung at and is not hit far.

tendon A tough band of tissue that connects muscle to bone.

triple A base hit that allows the batter to reach third base.

walk An advance to first base awarded a baseball player who during a turn at bat takes four pitches that are balls.

Baseball Canada

2212 Gladwin Crescent

Suite A7

Ottawa, ON K1B 5N1

Canada

(613) 748-5606

E-mail: info@baseball.ca

Web site: http://www.baseball.ca/eng_home.cfm

Federally incorporated in 1964 as the Canadian Federation of Amateur Baseball, Baseball Canada is the governing body for baseball in Canada and is made up of 10 provincial associations representing players, coaches, and umpires nationwide.

Canadian Baseball News

P.O. Box 73600

509 St. Clair Avenue West

Toronto, ON M6C 1C0

Canada

E-mail: info@canadianbaseballnews.com

Web site: http://www.canadianbaseballnews.com/Pages/abouCBN.html

Canadian Baseball News will keep you posted on all major events involving professional Canadian baseball teams, Canadian-born players, and former members of both the Toronto Blue Jays and the Montreal Expos.

Cincinnati Reds Hall of Fame

100 Main Street

Cincinnati, OH 45202

(513) 765-7576

Web site: http://cincinnati.reds.mlb.com/cin/ballpark/museum/index.jsp

The Cincinnati Reds Hall of Fame and Museum offers fans of the Reds, and of baseball, a comprehensive look into the sport's heralded past.

Ken Griffey Sr. Foundation

117 East Amelia Street

Orlando, FL 32801

(321) 256-4561

E-mail: dhutton31@hotmail.com

Web site: http://www.kengriffeysrfoundation.org

The Ken Griffey Sr. Foundation seeks to increase awareness about the need to adopt healthy lifestyles that include exercise and fitness in America's youth, in an effort to improve their quality of life and build better, stronger communities.

Little League International Baseball and Softball

539 U.S. Route 15 Highway

P.O. Box 3485

Williamsport, PA 17701-0485

(570) 326-1921

Web site: http://www.littleleague.org/Learn_More/About_Our_Organization/
contacts.htm

Little League Baseball, Incorporated, is a nonprofit organization whose mission is to "promote, develop, supervise, and voluntarily assist in all lawful ways, the interest of those who will participate in Little League Baseball and Softball."

Major League Baseball

Office of the Commissioner of Baseball

Allan H. (Bud) Selig, Commissioner

245 Park Avenue, 31st Floor

New York, NY 10167

(212) 931-7800

Web site: http://www.mlb.com

This is the operating organization for baseball's major leagues.

National Baseball Hall of Fame and Museum

25 Main Street

Cooperstown, NY 13326

1-888-HALL-OF-FAME

Web site: http://web.baseballhalloffame.org/index.jsp

This not-for-profit educational institution is dedicated to fostering an appreciation of the historical development of the game by preserving baseball memorabilia and honoring players who had exceptional careers.

Seattle Mariners

P.O. Box 4100
Seattle, WA 98194
(206) 346-4000
Web site: http://seattle.mariners.mlb.com/index.jsp?c_id = sea
This is the official organization and Web site for the Seattle Mariners.

WEB SITES

Due to the changing nature of Internet links, Rosen Publishing has developed an online list of Web sites related to the subject of this book. This site is updated regularly. Please use this link to access the list:

http://www.rosenlinks.com/sfam/grif

FOR FURTHER READING

Christopher, Matt. *At the Plate with Ken Griffey, Jr.* Boston, MA: Little, Brown Young Readers, 1997.

Griffey, Ken, Jr. *Junior: Griffey on Griffey*. New York, NY: HarperCollins, 1997.

Gutman, Bill. *Ken Griffey Jr.: A Biography*. New York, NY: Simon Spotlight Entertainment, 1998.

Joseph, Paul. *Awesome Athletes: Ken Griffey Jr*. Edina, MN: Checkerboard Books, 1997.

Kramer, Barbara. *Ken Griffey, Junior: All-Around All-Star*. Minneapolis, MN: Lerner Publications, 1996.

Press, Skip. *Star Families: Ken Griffey, Jr., & Ken Griffey, Sr.* Parsippany, NJ: Crestwood House, 1995.

Rolfe, John. *Sports Illustrated for Kids: Ken Griffey, Jr.* New York, NY: Sports Illustrated Books, 1999.

Savage, Jeff. *Sports Great: Ken Griffey, Jr.* Berkeley Heights, NJ: Enslow Publishers, Inc., 2000.

Sports Publishing. *101 Little Known Facts About Ken Griffey, Jr.* Champaign, IL: Sports Publishing, 1997.

Stewart, Mark. *Ken Griffey Jr.: All-American Slugger*. Danbury, CT: Children's Press, 1999.

BIBLIOGRAPHY

Associated Press. "Ken Griffey Jr. Dealt to White Sox." July 31, 2008. Retrieved March 1, 2009 (http://www.nydailynews.com/sports/baseball/2008/07/31/2008-07-31_ken_griffey_jr_dealt_to_white_sox.html).

Baker, Geoff. "The Kid Comes Home: Griffey Back Where His All-Star Career Began." *Seattle Times*, February 19, 2009. Retrieved March 1, 2009 (http://seattletimes.nwsource.com/html/sports/2008758659_griffeynew19.htm).

Cincinnati Vintage Baseball Club. "1869 Cincinnati Red Stockings Vintage Baseball Team." Retrieved March 1, 2009 (http://www.1869reds.com).

Famous Sports Stars. "Ken Griffey Jr.—Returned to Cincinnati, Struggled." Retrieved March 1, 2009 (http://sports.jrank.org/pages/1816/Griffey-Ken-Jr-Returned-Cincinnati-Struggled.html).

Fay, John. "Camp Griffey Now Complete: Senior Arrives; Jokes Begin." *Cincinnati Enquirer*, February 25, 2000. Retrieved March 1, 2009 (http://reds.enquirer.com/2000/02/25/red_camp_griffey_now.html).

Fayed, Lisa. "Ken Griffey Jr.'s Parents Diagnosed with Cancer." About.com: Cancer, February 26, 2009. Retrieved March 1, 2009 (http://cancer.about.com/od/celebritiesandcancer/a/kengriffeyjr.htm).

Frei, Terry. "Baseball's Golden Boy Once Despaired; Suicide Attempt Now Seems Silly." *Denver Post*, June 9, 1997, p. D.5.

Haft, Chris. "Fastest to 400: Griffey Sets Home Run Mark." *Cincinnati Enquirer*, April 11, 2000. Retrieved March 1, 2009 (http://reds.enquirer.com/2000/04/11/red_fastest_to_400.html).

Hatton, Spencer. "Junior's Back Where He Belongs." *Yakima Herald-Republic*, February 23, 2009, p. A.4.

Hickey, John. "Griffey's Return Creates a Buzz; 'Legend,' 'Hall of Famer' Among Mariners' Compliment." *Seattle Post-Intelligencer*, February 20, 2009, p. B.1.

Jackson, Tony. "Griffey Gives in Quiet Way; Dedication to Make-a-Wish Often Unseen Amid Troubles with Reds." *Seattle Post-Intelligencer*, March 7, 2002, p. C.3.

Jayne, Greg. "20 Fun Facts About Ken Griffey Jr." *Columbian*, June 23, 2007, p. B.8.

Kay, Joe. "Game of the Day: This Bash Is for You, Pops." *Seattle Times*, June 20, 2005, p. C.7.

Ken Griffey Sr. Foundation. "Biography of Ken Griffey Sr." Retrieved February 1, 2009 (http://www.kengriffeysrfoundation.org/board.html).

Ken Griffey Sr. Foundation. "Our Mission." Retrieved February 1, 2009 (http://www.kengriffeysrfoundation.org).

Los Angeles Times. "Griffey Delivers Again with a Big Father's Day." June 20, 2005, p. D.10.

Miller, Ted. "For Griffey, an Awkward Reconciliation of Sorts." *Seattle Post-Intelligencer*, June 23, 2007, p. E.1.

Nightengale, Bob. "Griffey's Days in Cincinnati May Be Numbered." *USA Today*, May 7, 2008. Retrieved March 1, 2009 (http://www.usatoday.com/sports/baseball/nl/reds/2008-05-05-griffey_N.htm).

Rhoden, William C. "For Griffey, What Could Have Been, and What May Be." *New York Times*, July 14, 2007, p. D.3.

Savage, Jeff. *Sports Great: Ken Griffey, Jr.* Berkeley Heights, NJ: Enslow Publishers, Inc., 2000.

Sheldon, Mark. "Family Watches Griffey's Historic Homer." MLB.com, June 10, 2008. Retrieved March 1, 2009 (http://mlb.mlb.com/news/article.jsp?ymd = 20080609&content_id = 2879059&vkey = news_cin&fext = .jsp&c_id = cin).

Sheldon, Mark. "Griffey Joins Kings of Clout with No. 600." MLB.com, June 10, 2008. Retrieved March 1, 2009 (http://mlb.mlb.com/news/article.jsp?ymd = 20080609&content_id = 2879002&vkey = news_cin&fext = .jsp&c_id = cin).

Sherwin, Bob. "Mariners Become Family Business—Ken Griffey Sr., 40, Joins Griffey Jr., 20, in Major League's First Father-Son Tandem." *Seattle Times*, August 29, 1990. Retrieved March 1, 2009 (http://community.seattletimes.nwsource.com/archive/?date = 19900829&slug = 1090222).

Silverleib, Alan. "Ken Griffey, Jr. Named Public Diplomacy Envoy." CNNPolitics.com, November 18, 2008. Retrieved March 1, 2009 (http://politicalticker.blogs.cnn.com/2008/11/18/ken-griffey-jr-named-public-diplomacy-envoy).

Sports Publishing. *101 Little Known Facts About Ken Griffey, Jr.* Champaign, IL: Sports Publishing, 1997.

Stone, Larry. "Ken Griffey Jr. Down & Out at Home." *Seattle Times*, June 16, 2002. Retrieved March 1, 2009 (http://community.seattletimes.nwsource.com/archive/?date=20020616&slug=griffey161).

TheBaseballPage.com. "Ken Griffey Sr." Retrieved February 1, 2009 (http://www.thebaseballpage.com/players/griffke01.php).

Torre, Pablo S. "Growing Up Griffey." *Sports Illustrated for Kids*, January/February 2009, Vol. 21, Issue 1, p. 40.

Wald, Bruce. "Banquet Honors Donora High Grad Ken Griffey Sr." *Pittsburgh Tribune-Review*, January 13, 2008. Retrieved March 1, 2009 (http://www.pittsburghlive.com/x/pittsburghtrib/news/mostread/s_546841.html).

Washington Post. "Griffey Finally Connects for 600th." June 10, 2008, p. E.6.

Yahoo! Sports. "Ken Griffey Jr.—Seattle Mariners." Retrieved February 24, 2009 (http://sports.yahoo.com/mlb/players/4305).

ABOUT THE AUTHOR

J. Elizabeth Mills is an author who has written numerous books for children. An avid sports fan, especially of the Pittsburgh Steelers, Pirates, and Penguins, she can't wait to see Ken Griffey Jr. play at Safeco Field. Mills lives in Seattle, Washington.

PHOTO CREDITS

Cover © Charles Franklin/MLB Photos via Getty Images; pp. 4–5, 10–11 © Ronald C. Modra/Sports Imagery/Getty Images; p. 7 © Ron Vesely/MLB Photos via Getty Images; p. 8 © Ken Levine/Allsport/Getty Images; p. 13 © Rob Tringali/Sportschrome/Getty Images; p. 16 © Jonathan Daniel/ Allsport/Getty Images; p. 17 © Rogers Photo Archive/Getty Images; pp. 19, 26, 35 © AP Photos; p. 21 © Michael Zagaris/MLB Photos via Getty Images; p. 24 © Peter Newcomb/AFP/Getty Images; p. 25 © Ezra Shaw/ Allsport/Getty Images; p. 29 © Eliot J. Schechter/Getty Images; pp. 32–33 Joe Robbins/Getty Images.

Designer: Les Kanturek; Editor: Bethany Bryan;
Photo Researcher: Marty Levick